Pebble®
Plus

Exploring the Galaxy

Earth

by Thomas K. Adamson

Consulting Editor: Gail Saunders-Smith, PhD

Consultant: James Gerard
Aerospace Education Specialist, NASA
Kennedy Space Center, Florida

CAPSTONE PRESS
a capstone imprint

Pebble Plus is published by Capstone Press,
151 Good Counsel Drive, P.O. Box 669, Mankato, Minnesota 56002.
www.capstonepub.com

042010
005760

Library of Congress Cataloging-in-Publication Data
Adamson, Thomas K., 1970–
    Earth / by Thomas K. Adamson.—Rev. and updated.
    p. cm.—(Pebble plus. Exploring the galaxy)
    Includes bibliographical references and index.
    ISBN-13: 978-1-4296-0731-5 (hardcover)
    ISBN-13: 978-1-4296-5809-6 (saddle-stitched)
    1. Earth—Juvenile literature. I. Title. II. Series.
QB631.4.A33 2008
525—dc22   2007004450

Summary: Simple text and photographs describe planet Earth.

Editorial Credits
Mari C. Schuh, editor; Kia Adams, designer; Alta Schaffer, photo researcher

Photo Credits
Bruce Coleman Inc./Phil Degginger, 16–17
Corbis Images, 19
Digital Vision, 5 (Venus)
Digital Wisdom, 13
Image Source, 20–21
NASA, 1; JPL, 5 (Jupiter); JPL/Caltech, 5 (Uranus); NSSDC, 15
PhotoDisc Inc., cover, 4 (Neptune), 5 (Mars, Mercury, Earth, Sun, Saturn), 7 (both), 8–9; PhotoDisc Imaging, 11

Note: When Earth is viewed from space, Earth's north is not always oriented "up."

Note to Parents and Teachers

The Exploring the Galaxy set supports national science standards related to earth science. This book describes and illustrates the planet Earth. The photographs support early readers in understanding the text. The repetition of words and phrases helps early readers learn new words. This book also introduces early readers to subject-specific vocabulary words, which are defined in the Glossary section. Early readers may need assistance to read some words and to use the Table of Contents, Glossary, Read More, Internet Sites, and Index sections of the book.

Table of Contents

Earth

Earth is the only planet
in the solar system where
people and animals live.
Earth and the other planets
move around the Sun.

The Solar System

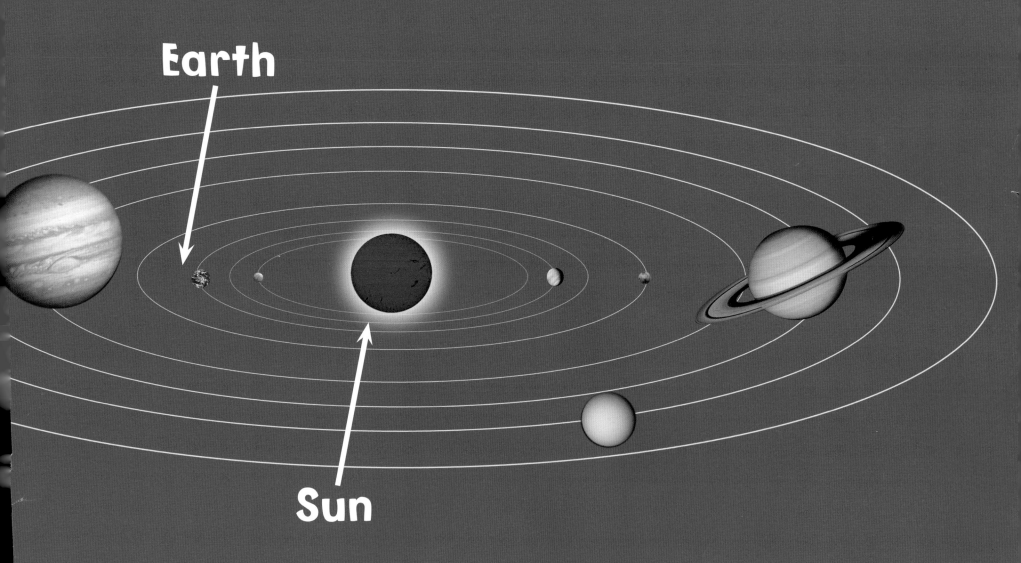

Earth

Sun

It takes about 365 days

for Earth to move around

the Sun one time.

Earth moves around the Sun

once each year.

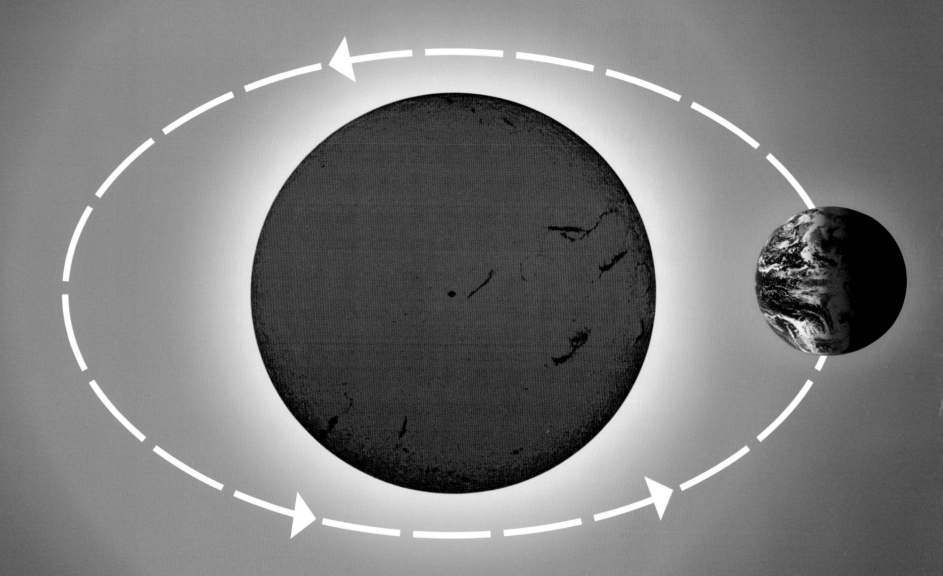

Air and Land

People and animals

breathe the air on Earth.

Life cannot survive

without air.

9

Earth is made
of rock and metal.
The center of Earth
is hot molten metal.

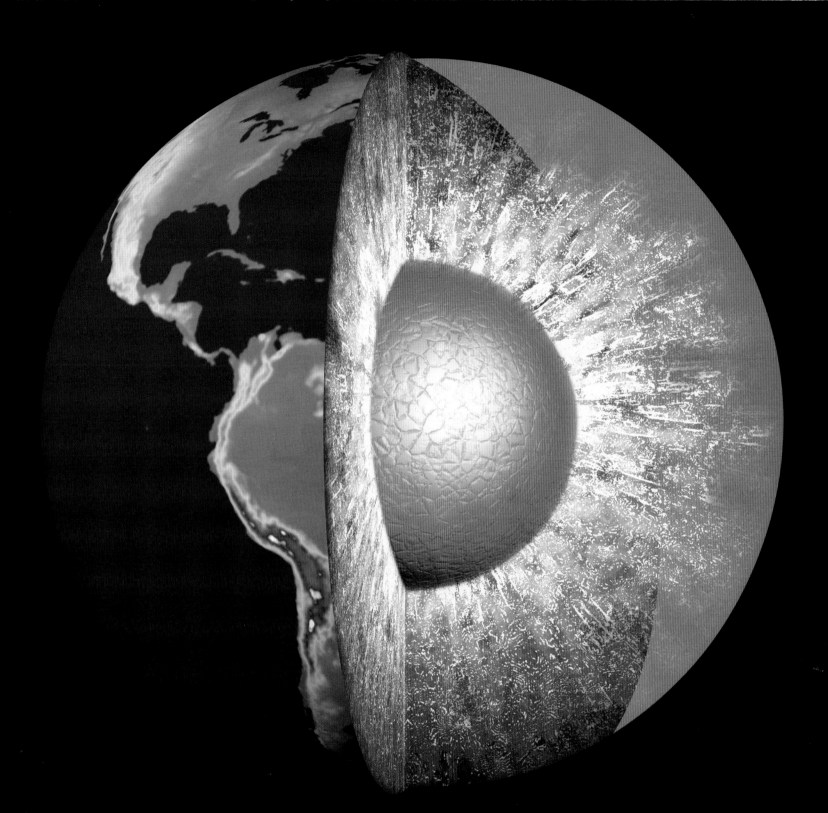

Water and Weather

Water covers most

of Earth's surface.

People and animals

cannot live without water.

Most of Earth's water

is in the oceans.

The water makes

Earth look blue from space.

Earth has many
types of weather.
Different places on Earth
get different kinds of weather.

People and Earth

Earth has one moon.

People can easily see
the Moon from Earth.

Earth gives

people and animals

all they need to live.

Earth has air, food, water,

and the right temperature.

Glossary

breathe—to take air in and out of the lungs; people and animals must breathe to live.

molten—melted by heat

moon—an object that moves around a planet; Earth has one moon.

ocean—a large body of salt water; the five oceans of Earth are the Atlantic, Pacific, Arctic, Antarctic, and Indian Oceans.

planet—a large object that moves around the Sun; Earth is the third planet from the Sun; there are eight planets in the solar system.

Sun—the star that the planets move around; the Sun provides light and heat for the planets.

weather—the conditions outside; weather can be hot or cold, wet or dry, calm or windy, or clear or cloudy.

year—the period of time in which Earth makes one trip around the Sun; one year is about 365 days.

Read More

Kortenkamp, Steve. *Why Isn't Pluto a Planet?: A Book About Planets.* First Facts: Why in the World? Mankato, Minn.: Capstone Press, 2007.

Richardson, Adele. *Earth.* First Facts: The Solar System. Mankato, Minn.: Capstone Press, 2008.

Wimmer, Teresa. *Earth.* My First Look at Planets. Mankato, Minn.: Creative Education, 2007.

Internet Sites

FactHound offers a safe, fun way to find Internet sites related to this book. All of the sites on FactHound have been researched by our staff.

Here's how:

1. Visit *www.facthound.com*

2. Choose your grade level.

3. Type in this book ID **9781429607315** for age-appropriate sites. You may also browse subjects by clicking on letters, or by clicking on pictures and words.

4. Click on the **Fetch It** button.

FactHound will fetch the best sites for you!

Index

Word Count: 148
Grade: 1
Early-Intervention Level: 15